Pump and Pedal

by Natalie Lambert
illustrated by Meryl Henderson

Core Decodable 55

McGraw Hill Education

Bothell, WA • Chicago, IL • Columbus, OH • New York, NY

MHEonline.com

Send all inquiries to:
McGraw-Hill Education
8787 Orion Place
Columbus, OH 43240

ISBN: 978-0-02-145648-2
MHID: 0-02-145648-8

Printed in the United States of America.

9 10 11 12 KOD 24

Pump fast at the signal, Pat.
Pedal to get ahead.

A big hill is not a problem.
Just pump and pedal.

Pump past a garden and maple trees.
Pedal next to the dog kennel.

Pedal under the metal bridge.
Pump fast in the tunnel.

Pump in Fossil Park.
Pedal! Pedal! Pedal!

Pump to a fast finish.
Win a medal, Pat!